HEARING

A TRUE BOOK®

by

Patricia J. Murphy

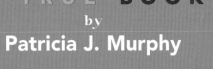

Children's Press®
A Division of Scholastic Inc.

New York Toronto London Auckland Sydney
Mexico City New Delhi Hong Kong
Danbury, Connecticut

Your ears are the key to your sense of hearing.

Reading Consultant
Nanci R. Vargus, Ed.D.
Assistant Professor
Literacy Education
University of Indianapolis
Indianapolis, IN

Content Consultant
Beth Cox
Science Learning Specialist
Horry County Schools
Conway, SC

Dedication:
For my sister, Elizabeth

Library of Congress Cataloging-in-Publication Data

Murphy, Patricia J., 1963–
  Hearing / by Patricia J. Murphy.
    p. cm. — (A True book)
    Includes bibliographical references and index.
    Contents: Now hear this!—Through the outer and inner ears—On to the inner ear—When ears cannot hear—Take good care of your ears. 2731 1207 3/03
    ISBN 0-516-22599-5 (lib. bdg.)   0-516-26970-4 (pbk.)
1. Hearing—Juvenile literature. 2. Ear—Juvenile literature. [1. Hearing. 2. Ear. 3. Senses and sensation.] I. Title. II. Series.
QP462.2 .M875 2003
612.8'5—dc21
                                        2001008323

1 2 3 4 5 6 7 8 9 10 R 12 11 10 09 08 07 06 05 04 03

Contents

Your sense of hearing enables you to listen to a friend tell you a secret.

Now Hear This!

Your ears stick outside of your head for thousands of reasons. These reasons are sounds. Your ears hear the whisper of a friend or the ring of an ice cream truck because sounds collected by your outer ears.

Sounds are carried by waves made up of air molecules.

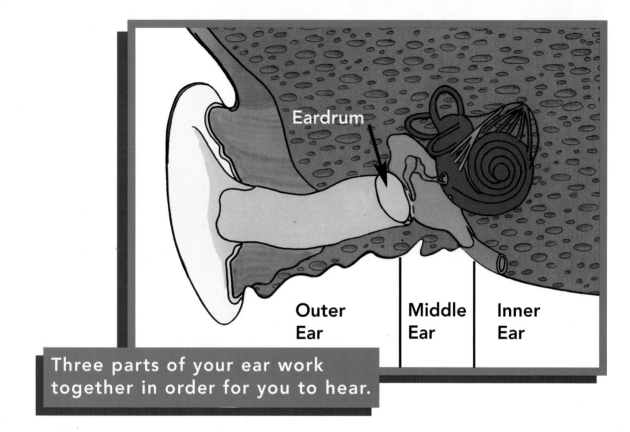

Eardrum

Outer Ear

Middle Ear

Inner Ear

Three parts of your ear work together in order for you to hear.

These air molecules carry sounds through solids, liquids, and gases. The molecules begin to vibrate or move back and forth and bump into other molecules. They carry the sound through the three parts of the ear. These three parts are your outer ear, middle ear, and inner ear.

When you hear your favorite song, sound waves first travel through your outer ear's **auricle**

Your outer ear is the first part used in the hearing process.

and then through your ear canal. The sound waves must travel along the 1-inch (2.5-centimeter) long ear canal to get to the eardrum, or tympanic membrane. As the sound waves strike the eardrum, the eardrum starts to vibrate. Once the eardrum starts to vibrate, it moves the middle ear's three little bones: the hammer (malleus), anvil (incus), and stirrup (stapes). Then, these

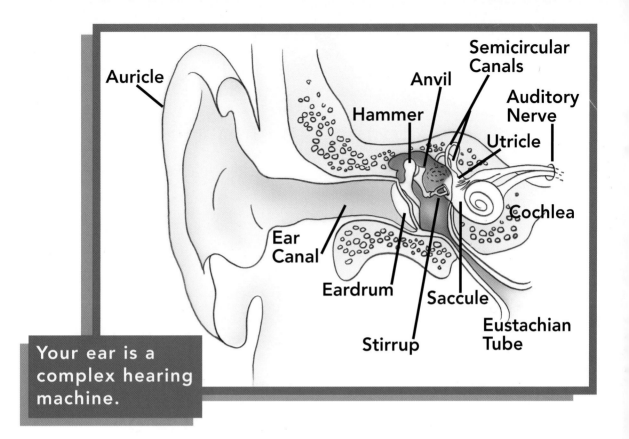

Auricle

Anvil

Semicircular Canals

Hammer

Auditory Nerve

Utricle

Ear Canal

Cochlea

Eardrum

Saccule

Stirrup

Eustachian Tube

Your ear is a complex hearing machine.

vibrations move on to the inner ear.

The inner ear's **cochlea** changes these vibrations into nerve messages, or impulses. The cochlea sends these nerve impulses along the auditory nerve to the brain. In the brain, these impulses travel to the auditory cortex. This is the part of the brain where hearing happens.

Other parts of the inner ear help keep you standing tall. The semicircular canals, **utricle**, and **saccule** keep your head and body balanced. Without these parts, you might have trouble moving around or you might lose your balance and fall. When you move up and down, side to side, or other ways, these structures

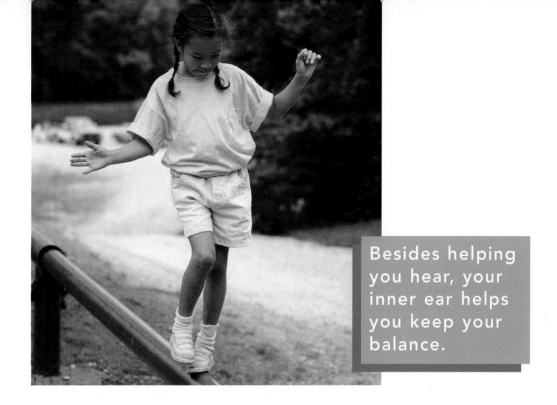

make sure you do not fall.
They do this by sending nerve
impulses to your body's muscles. These nerve impulses tell
your muscles to make quick
changes to keep your body
upright or moving ahead.

The semicircular canals contain fluid and hair receptor cells. Any movement of the head makes the fluid swirl and the hair receptor cells bend. When this happens, the hair receptor cells send messages to the brain. A message might tell the brain, "Head is moving to the right!"

The utricle and saccule have tiny hairs with jellylike coating. These hairs pick up changes in motion and in **gravity**. Together, the semicircular

This close-up photograph shows the hairs in the inner ear.

canals, utricle, and saccule work with receptors in the eyes, muscles, and ligaments. You couldn't keep your balance if any one of these were not working.

Through the Outer and Middle Ear

Like a team, your outer ear and middle ear work together. The outer ear, or auricle, catches the sound waves. It sends these waves along the ear canal to the eardrum.

When sound waves move through the canal, they must

Baseball players listen to their coach. They work together, much like your outer and middle ear.

pass through the canal's helpful hairs and sticky wax called cerumen. The hairs and earwax make sure only sound waves get through to the eardrum. They keep dirt, bugs, and other things from entering and hurting the rest of the ear.

The middle ear is filled with air. Its **eustachian tube** connects the middle ear to the back of your throat. This tube

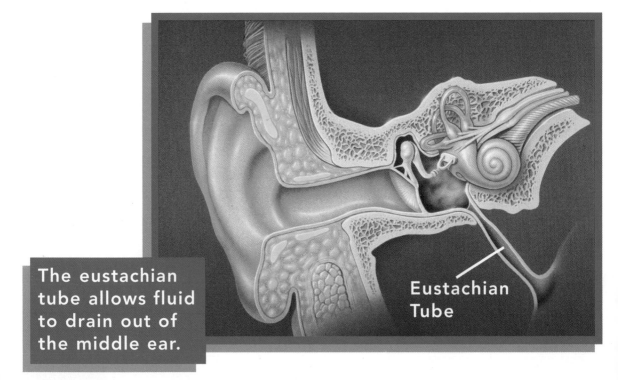

The eustachian tube allows fluid to drain out of the middle ear.

Eustachian Tube

allows extra fluid in the middle ear to drain down the throat. It also protects the delicate parts of the middle ear.

The eustachian tube allows air to flow into and out of the middle ear. This keeps the **air pressure** inside and outside the ear the same. If these pressures were different, the eardrum could not work properly and could burst.

After traveling through the ear canal, sound waves strike

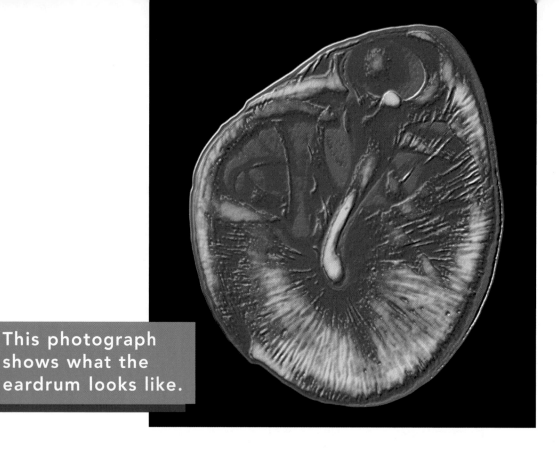

This photograph shows what the eardrum looks like.

the ear's eardrum. The eardrum separates the outer ear from the middle ear. The sound waves that move back and forth upon the top of the eardrum start the middle ear's tiny bones vibrating. Each of the bones is connected to the next bone by ligaments. As one bone vibrates, it makes the others move back and forth.

As the vibrations pass through the eardrum to the bones, they move more and more. They become more amplified, or louder. When the eardrum starts to move, it starts the hammer vibrating. The hammer's movement starts the anvil vibrating. Next, the anvil

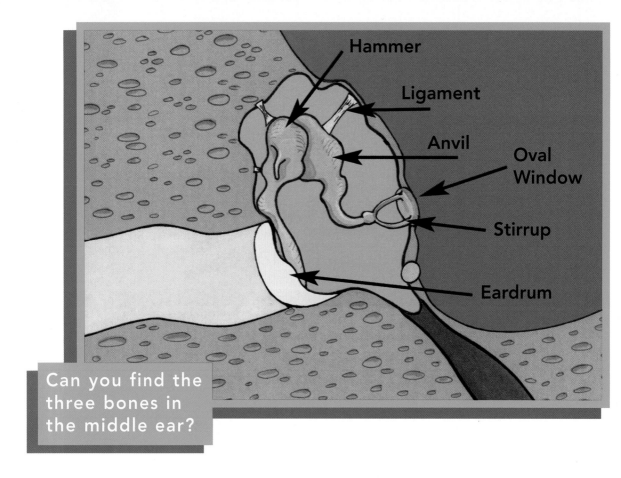

Hammer

Ligament

Anvil

Oval Window

Stirrup

Eardrum

Can you find the
three bones in
the middle ear?

starts the stirrup moving.
Then, the stirrup vibrates the
oval window. The oval window
is the door that leads to the
inner ear.

On to the Inner Ear!

The inner ear is like the launching pad to the hearing world. It is the last stop before sounds make their way to the brain so you can hear. The inner ear's oval window stands waiting for the middle ear's vibrations to arrive. It counts on the middle ear's stirrup to

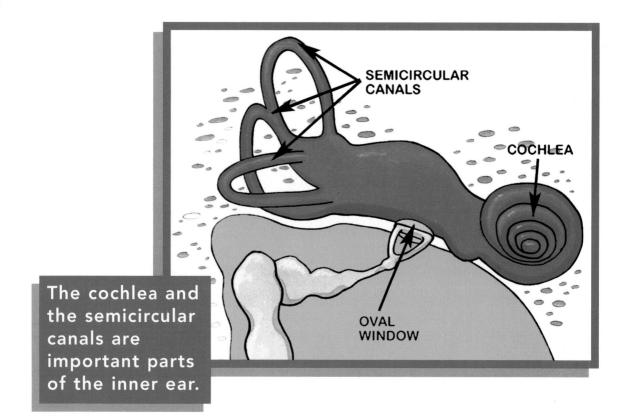

SEMICIRCULAR
CANALS

COCHLEA

OVAL
WINDOW

The cochlea and the semicircular canals are important parts of the inner ear.

vibrate it. The oval window is the opening to the inner ear's cochlea. The cochlea is made of three connecting tubes and looks like a seashell.

Each of the tubes is filled with liquid. Along the bottom

of the cochlea's tubes, there is a layer of tiny sensory hairs, or nerve cells. This strip is called the organ of Corti. When the oval window begins to move, the vibrations create

This photograph provides a close-up look at the tiny hairs on the organ of Corti inside your inner ear.

waves in the inner ear's liquid. These waves make the cochlea's tiny sensory hairs move. When the tiny hairs begin to move, they change the vibrations into nerve messages or impulses.

Each of the hair cells reacts to a different sound **frequency**. Frequency is the number of vibrations per second of sound. Frequency determines the pitch, or highness or lowness of a sound. Nerve impulses are sent along the hairs' nerve

A sound with a high frequency has a high pitch, such as someone scraping nails on a chalkboard. A sound with a low frequency has a low pitch, such as a truck rumbling down a street.

fibers. They leave the cochlea as special coded messages. Then, they are sent along the ear's auditory nerve. The auditory nerve is the bundle of nerves at the bottom of the cochlea. It

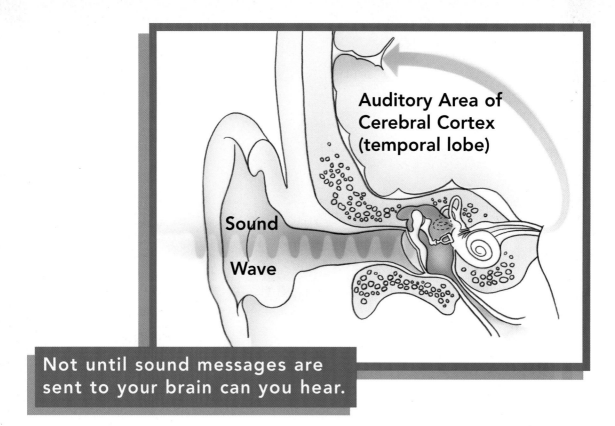

Auditory Area of
Cerebral Cortex
(temporal lobe)

Sound

Wave

Not until sound messages are
sent to your brain can you hear.

sends the ear's nerve impulses to
the auditory cortex of the brain.
This is the area in the temporal
lobe of your brain where the
messages are received and iden-
tified as sounds. At last, you hear!

The Audiologist

An audiologist is someone who finds and fixes hearing problems. Audiologists test people to see if they can hear and sort out different sounds. They also help people hear better by giving them hearing aids and other tools. To become audiologists, people must go to college. After college, they must study one to two more years. When they finish school, they must pass special tests.

When Ears Can't Hear

What are your favorite sounds? Imagine not being able to hear them. What would it be like? If you had a hearing problem, sounds might be too low or unclear for you to understand. You may not hear any sounds at all. Hearing problems can affect the ear's job of collecting and

Imagine if you couldn't hear your favorite music or the voice of your best friend (above). A nurse uses special equipment to check a baby's ability to hear (right).

sending information to the brain. There are two kinds of hearing loss called conductive hearing loss and sensorineural hearing loss.

Conductive hearing loss lessens the volume of sound an ear can hear. This loss is often caused by ear infections. It can also occur with a buildup of earwax in the ear canal.

Bacteria from the nose and throat can enter the ear through the eustachian tube and cause an infection. When bacteria or germs build up in the middle ear, it makes the ear canal become red, swollen, and filled with liquid or pus. This swelling and liquid

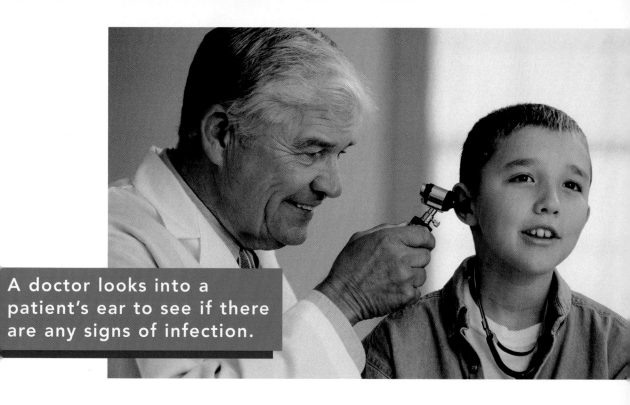

A doctor looks into a patient's ear to see if there are any signs of infection.

keep the eardrum and bones in the middle ear from doing their best work.

Some doctors give people medicine to get rid of their ear infections. Doctors may treat recurring ear infections by putting small tubes inside one or both of the eardrums. These tubes—the size of rice grains—help keep air in the ear and liquid and bacteria out. They act like mini-Eustachian tubes. Doctors also use water and special tools to remove buildups of earwax.

Conductive hearing problems can be helped with medicine, surgery, or hearing aids. Hearing aids are like tiny computers placed in the ear. They use small microphones to pick up sounds and make them louder. Then

A student uses a hearing aid to hear better in class.

they use small speakers to send the sound back to the ear. Hearing aids do not fix lost hearing. They make sounds louder so that they can be detected by the hearing that remains.

Sensorineural hearing loss keeps people from being able to hear sound clearly. It is caused by problems with the cochlea or the auditory nerve. Many people who are born deaf have this type of hearing loss. Loud noises and injuries to the head can also cause this type of loss. In this hearing loss, the brain is unable to receive nerve impulses. The ears' tiny sensory hairs do not work. This stops nerve messages or impulses from traveling to the brain.

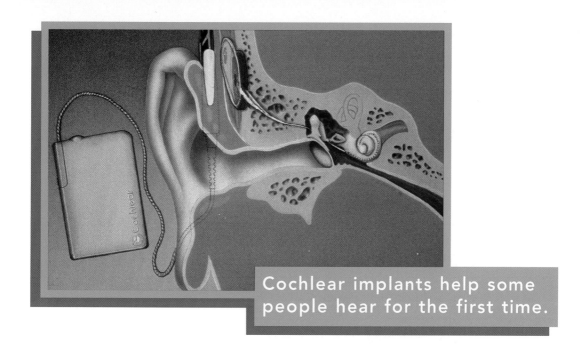

Cochlear implants help some people hear for the first time.

Today, cochlear implants help people with sensorineural hearing loss. These mini-computers are placed behind a person's ears. They are able to break down sounds into different frequencies. Small **sensors** are placed in the cochlea. Cochlear implants help the cochlea send its nerve impulses to the brain. In many cases, these implants help people hear. For some, the implants allow them to hear for the first time.

Scientists hope to find other ways to help people who have hearing loss or are deaf. Until then, people who cannot hear must use their other senses to help them. Some read lips to understand others or use American Sign Language to communicate. Others may have

Many deaf people use American Sign Language to communicate (above). There are also machines that enable deaf people to use the telephone (right).

special dogs that alert them to noises. They may also use special lights to alert them to smoke alarms or alarm clocks. They can do many things to help them with their daily lives.

A Second Pair of Ears!

Thanks to special hearing dogs, people with hearing loss can "hear" what is going on around them. These specially trained dogs alert people with hearing loss to everyday sounds, such as doorbells, kitchen timers, smoke alarms, and sirens. Once the dogs are trained, they meet with their masters. Together, they go through more training. The masters learn how to recognize when their dogs are calling attention to important sounds.

Hearing dogs let their owners know when a doorbell rings or an alarm goes off.

Take Good Care of Your Ears

It is no wonder that most of your ear is tucked away in a safe hiding place. Your ears are the most fragile sense organs that you have. Any harm done to your ears cannot be fixed. There are many things, however, that you can do to save your hearing.

• Turn down the music! Do not listen to loud music. If you cannot hear your voice over the music, the music is too loud. The louder the noise, the less time it takes to damage your ears' hair cells.

• If you attend music concerts or sporting events, wear earplugs. Earplugs are made from hard foam rubber. They are placed between your outer ear and ear canal.

• Play personal stereos at medium or low volumes. Remember that there is only 1 inch (2.5 cm) of space from your external ear to your eardrum for sound to travel.

• Do you play sports? Wear a helmet! Athletes who box, wrestle, or play any physical sport can hurt their outer ears.

Be good to your ears by cleaning them regularly.

• Keep your ears clean. Wash only the outside rims and behind your ears. The rest of your ear cleans itself!

• Visit an ear doctor when you have a wax buildup, an ear infection, or a health problem that affects your hearing.

If you follow these tips, your ears will hear for many years!

Facts About Hearing

- An adult brain can identify as many as 500,000 sounds.

- Each cochlea has more than twenty thousand nerve hairs or cells.

- Earplugs reduce loud noises and the chance of hearing loss.

- Your ears hear sounds twenty-four hours a day. However, when you sleep, you don't hear them.

- The hammer, anvil, and stirrup are the smallest bones in your body.

- You can thank your parents for the external shape of your ears. The shape of a person's ears runs in the family!

- People pay little attention to certain sounds. This is called selective hearing.

- Sensorineural hearing loss is the most common type of hearing loss.

- One in one thousand babies is born with hearing loss.

To Find Out More

Here are some additional resources to help you learn more about the sense of hearing:

Books

Arnold, Caroline. **Did You Hear That?** Charlesbridge, 2001.

Ballard, Carol. **How Do Our Ears Hear?** Austin, TX, Raintree/Steck Vaughn, 1998.

Cobb, Vicki. **Perk Up Your Ears: Discover Your Sense of Hearing.** Millbrook Press, 2001.

Furgang, Kathy. **My Ears.** PowerKids Press, Inc., 2001.

Hurwitz, Sue. **Hearing.** PowerKids Press, 1997.

Pluckrose, Henry. **Listening and Hearing.** Raintree/ Steck Vaughn, 1998.

Pringle, Laurence. **Explore Your Senses: Hearing.** Benchmark Books, 2000.

Royston, Angela. **My World of Senses: Sound.** Chicago, IL, Heinemann Library, 2001.

Organizations and Online Sites

American Hearing Foundation
55 E. Washington Street, Suite 2022
Chicago, IL 60602

This organization provides information on hearing.

The Better Hearing Institute
http://www.betterhearing.org

Learn how to be better to your ears with the Better Hearing Institute's online site.

Handspeak
http://www.handspeak.com

Learn hundreds of American Sign Language words and phases. Animated movies show you how to move your hands.

Let's Hear It for the Ear!
http://www.kidshealth.org/ kid/body/ear_noSW.html

Find out what's new with the ear and other body parts on this kids' health site.

Seeing, Hearing, and Smelling the World
http://www.hhmi.org/senses/

Discover more about seeing, hearing, smelling, and more.

Sight & Hearing Association
674 Transfer Road
St. Paul, MN 55114-1402
http://www.sightandhearing. org

Learn how to conserve your hearing.

The Soundry
http://www.library.thinkquest. org/19537/Main.html?tqskip1= 1tqtime=1007

Learn more about sound and how we hear it on this educational site.

Important Words

air pressure the weight of the air pressing down on Earth

auricle the outer part of the ear

cochlea the area of the inner ear in which vibrations are turned into nerve impulses

eustachian tube the tube that connects the middle ear to the throat. It drains fluid, allows air in, and keeps the pressure inside and outside the ear the same

frequency the number of vibrations per second of sound, it is also called pitch

gravity the force that Earth has on objects in space; it pulls them toward Earth

saccule one of two areas in the semicircular canals that senses gravity and position of the head

sensor an instrument that picks up signals and sends them to another device or tool

utricle one of two areas in the semicircular canals that senses gravity and position of the head

Index

Meet the Author

Patricia J. Murphy writes children's storybooks, non-fiction books, early readers, and poetry. She also writes for magazines, corporations, educational publishing companies, and museums. Murphy lives in Northbrook, IL. She loves the sounds of rustling leaves and the crunch of snow under her boots!